BACKYARD HOMESTEADING:
Vegetable Gardening Basics

Table of Contents

Introduction

Conclusion

INTRODUCTION

According to the Farmer's Almanac, a vegetable garden of only 160 square feet can feed a family of four for six months. And, the produce that comes out of your garden can be organic, pesticide free, and ripened on the vine, unlike grocery store produce that is usually pesticide laden, picked green, and grown from genetically modified seeds.

Welcome to *Backyard Homesteading: Vegetable Gardening Basics*! This guide will provide you with the knowledge to start and successfully grow your own backyard vegetable garden. I'll help you figure out what type of vegetable garden is best for you and your yard. We'll discuss how to get your soil ready for planting, how to keep your plants healthy, and how to keep critters and pests away from your vegetables. When you finish reading this book, you'll know (among many other things):

- How to select the best spot in your yard for your garden (Chapter 1).
- How to maximize a shady yard for vegetable gardening (Chapter 1).
- The pros and cons of ground gardening and raised beds (Chapter 2).
- How to select the best varieties of vegetables for your garden (Chapter 3).
- How to transplant, seed-start, and direct sow your plants (Chapter 3).
- Easy preventive measures to help keep plants healthy and pest free (Chapter 4).
- Easy organic solutions to deal with pests and plant disease. (Chapter 4).
- How to use green manure to improve soil quality (Chapter 5).
- Easy methods to protecting garden soil from erosion in winter months. (Chapter 5)

I've maintained my own vegetable gardens for many years. During that time, I've learned a few garden secrets that I'll be sharing with you, like simple methods to decrease garden weeds and how to water your plants in a way that discourages mold and mildew from forming on plant leaves. I'll let you know why soil testing is so very important. In fact, just promise me you'll get your garden soil tested right now, and you can quickly skim my soil testing diatribe.

The information in this guide is presented in a manner that will be most useful for new vegetable gardeners. The information is easy-to-follow and entertaining, so your desire to garden will not be crushed by reading an incomprehensible, dry gardening guide. Technical gardening jargon is limited and any usage of technical gardening terms is followed by a simple explanation that will have you speaking garden-geek in no time.

So, let's snap to it, shall we? We'll start with designing your garden, then talk about getting your garden prepped, move on to planting, provide coping strategies for pest and plant issues, and finally talk about harvesting and winterizing your garden.

You didn't know about winterizing your garden?

Well, that's why you're here, right?

CHAPTER 1
YOUR GARDEN PLOT:
STARTING A VEGETABLE GARDEN

You can picture it, can't you?   Your very own kitchen garden. A place where you can plant and harvest and putter around and grow fresh vegetables, juicy berries, and aromatic herbs.

But, you wonder, how do you get started? Where should you put your garden? In that unused corner of your yard that's presently an extra patch of lawn that you have to pay the neighbor's son to randomly mow? Or, should your garden go in the small side yard that's presently a jumble of kids' bikes and old toys? Will your soil work for a garden? Your flowerbeds seem grow flowers, so the soil should be fine, right? What about watering? What's the best way to water a large amount of garden space?

Just how do you get a vegetable garden growing?

Starting a vegetable garden is probably easier than you think. First, you just need to pick the best spot in your yard to plant your garden, and the best spot is the spot that gets the best sunlight. It's also helpful if the area is protected from pets or other animals (or, is as protected as it can be) and has easy access to a water faucet.

Choosing a Space for Your Garden

Most vegetable plants require a minimum of 6-8 hours of sunlight per day, so it's important to choose a sunny spot in your yard for your garden. If your yard is short on sunny space (like mine), you can still make a garden work, but you may be a bit more limited in what you can get to grow. To maximize a shady yard, consider:

- What type of shade are you up against? Is the shade light or dappled (sunlight filtered through tree branches, for example)? Or, is the shade partial (receives direct sunlight for 3-5 hours per day)? Or, are you dealing with full shade (area receives little or no direct sunlight)?

  Some shade is easier to work with than others. Light or dappled shade still provides garden beds with a good amount of bright light, so you can still plant flowering vegetables, like peppers and squash, in these spots. Your plant yields won't be as high as they would be in full sun, but the plants will still produce.

  During the height of summer, partial shade can be great for growing vegetables that prefer cooler weather, such as beans, peas, and broccoli. Root vegetables, like radishes and carrots, tolerate partial shade fairly well. Leafy greens, like lettuce and chard, and herbs will grow in as little as three hours of sunlight per day.

- If your shade problems are caused by trees, consider trimming low-hanging branches, so more sunlight can filter through the canopy.
- Likely, your garden won't be completely sunny nor completely shady. Plan your garden so that your sun-loving veggies, like tomatoes and corn, are in the sunniest spots. Plant your

legumes in dappled light, and your root and leafy greens in your shadier spots.

- You can use reflective materials to increase the amount of indirect sunlight plants receive. Some gardeners place aluminum sheets along their garden fence to reflect extra light at their plants. You can also fill in the area around your garden beds with a light or white colored gravel to increase the amount of reflected sunlight.

  There are even reflective mulches available that you can spread around your plants, such as red plastic mulch for tomatoes. The mulch reflects the sunlight back at the plant's leaves and encourages photosynthesis which increases plant production. Many of these mulches have the added benefit of deterring garden pests like snails and aphids.

Other considerations when choosing your garden plot include:

- Access to water.

  Your garden will need to be watered frequently, sometimes daily when temperatures are high or the plants are producing. So, it may advantageous to have a spigot nearby to keep from hauling long hoses to and fro across your yard.

  Also, if you're considering using a home drip irrigation system for watering your garden, you'll need a good access point for the system.

- Protection from pets and other animals.

  Digging is your dog's favorite hobby right after sleeping and chasing squirrels. Pets just can't seem to resist burrowing in that cool soil when temperatures soar. You'll save yourself the aggravation of discovering Fido amid a pile of excavated cucumber plants if you can place your garden in an area that's already fenced off (like a side yard) or an area that easily can be (like a corner of the backyard).

Fencing can also help deter other animals, such as deer, rabbits, cats, and skunks.

After you've selected your garden space, you can have your soil tested to assess the health of your garden soil. You may be tempted to skip this step. I once did. And, after my vegetable plants failed to produce more than a handful of vegetables, I tested my soil. The results revealed that my garden soil was highly acidic; so much so that I'm surprised I didn't suffer acid burns while weeding.

Soil Testing

Before starting your garden, I highly advise getting your soil tested. Soil testing is relatively inexpensive, especially when you compare the cost of a soil test against the money and time you'll spend cultivating plants that just won't grow in nutrient poor soil.

Professional soil tests will give you the most accurate picture of your soil's health. A professional test will provide you with your garden soil's pH level (to within a tenth of one pH unit) as well as the amounts of phosphorous, potassium, calcium, nitrogen, and other nutrients in your soil. You'll also be provided with specific recommendations for improving your soil for the plants you want to grow. Most city and county extension offices and agricultural schools offer soil testing for a small fee.

There are also home soil test kits you can buy online or at most gardening stores. These kits are generally cheaper than professional tests, but they won't be as accurate. However, they'll at least give you a baseline measure as to the health of your soil.

To get an accurate soil reading, follow all directions of the professional tests and home test kits. You'll likely need to collect soil samples from multiple areas in your yard or garden. Once you have the results of your soil test, you can correct any nutrient deficiencies in your soil.

- Most vegetable plants like their soil slightly acidic. To increase soil acidity, you can add sulfur or aluminum sulfate to the soil. If your soil is too acidic, you can mix lime into the soil to raise the pH level. Generally, the soil in moist climates is more acidic while the soil in dry climates tends to be more alkaline.

Try to correct soil pH before sowing your garden. Add high amounts of lime or sulfur into the soil after your plants are in the ground, and you risk killing your plants. In fact, these supplements are best added to the soil 3-4 weeks before planting.

■ There are a number of mulches and fertilizers you can use to add nutrients, like calcium or phosphorus, back into the soil. Many are plant specific, so pay attention to labels. To keep your plants healthy and producing throughout your growing season, it's a good idea to fertilize on a regular basis.

There are also several easy home options for improving the quality of your soil. Egg shells are a good source of calcium. Epsom salts can provide your plants with magnesium. Kelp or seaweed, if you leave near the ocean, will add potassium to your soil. And, vegetable plants love coffee grounds, which makes a great deal of sense.

Aren't we all more productive once we've had a little coffee?

Chapter 2
Hoedown:
Prepping Your Garden

You've selected your garden space, a prime sunny area in the corner of your yard that, until now, has just been an extension of your lawn. But, what's the best way to turn this ground into a producing garden? How do you go from hard-packed lawn to tomatoes and beans and corn and peas? You have two options: a ground garden or raised beds.

Ground Gardening

Ground gardening, or row-cropping, is probably what pops into your mind when you think about a garden: long furrowed, rows carved straight into the earth. A ground garden is the consummate traditional garden.

Ground gardeners rave about the ease and flexibility of their method. There's no infrastructure involved; plants go straight into the tilled earth. Ground gardens require less water and less fertilizing since plant roots aren't subject to the restricted environment of a raised bed. And, gardens can easily be expanded, by tilling additional soil, or dismantled and replanted as lawn, if needed.

Ground gardens, however, do have their drawbacks. The soil in the ground will warm up later in the spring and cool down quicker in the fall. If you live in a warm climate, this isn't an issue. But, if you live in an area with late freezes and early frosts, ground gardens will give you a shorter growing season than raised beds. Ground gardens tend to take up more space which can be problematic in small yards, and ground gardens are more likely to be tromped on by children, pets, or klutzy gardeners (like me).

Also, unlike raised bed gardens, ground gardens are subject to the soil in your yard. If you're very, very lucky, you have a yard that has healthy soil, perfect for growing a vegetable garden. If you're more like the rest of us, your soil will likely need a little help in achieving the proper garden soil pH and the correct combination of soil nutrients.

That soil test you promised me you'd get will let you know what you need to add to your soil.

When constructing a ground garden:

- Break-up the soil at least one foot deep (a foot-and-half would be even better).

   This can be accomplished by rototilling or good, old fashioned shoveling. Remove any rocks and roots. The soil should be an even silty, consistency when you're finished. You can use a pitchfork to aerate the soil and break apart large clumps of dirt. A pitchfork is also handy in breaking through rock-hard topsoil.

- Enrich your garden soil before planting.

   Work compost and fertilizer into the soil. One of the best fertilizers to start with is herbivore animal manure. Cow and horse manures are commonly used, as are manures from chickens or rabbits. Bat dung or bat guano is one of the best fertilizers you can use, but it's more expensive than other options.

Before using animal manure, make sure it's been property aged (dried) or composted. Never use droppings from carnivorous animals, like dogs or cats.

- Level soil to avoid water runoff and drainage issues.

Rake through soil before planting. This is better accomplished with a bow rake (a metal rake with wide spaced tines) rather than a leaf rake, which will catch and pull soil towards you. For easy leveling, flip the bow rake over and use the flat, non-tine side to smooth the earth.

- Create a garden plan and construct rows and beds accordingly.

Decide which vegetables you'd like to plant ahead of time, so you can choose their spot in your garden. Hoe rows for corn, beans, peas, and other row crops now and also create the beds and mounds for your tomatoes, squash, melons, or cucumbers. This way, you'll know where everything is going before you start planting and you can make any adjustments necessary. It's much easier to rearrange your garden while it's still just earth than after there are seeds and plants in the ground.

Leave enough space between your crops, so that you can easily move around and tend to your plants. You can mulch between beds to help cut back on weeds.

Ground gardens are more likely to get trampled by children and pets, so if you can't fence off your garden, consider using a small border to mark off the garden space to serve as a reminder for kids and a training tool for dogs. Hopefully, your dogs are smarter and more open to training than mine.

There are all types of borders available for purchase: brick, stone, wood, and plastic. You can also use all of those rocks you dug out of your garden patch to create a border. Cost efficient and helps you get rid of a large pile of rocks.

Raised Beds

Raised bed gardening has grown in popularity in recent years. Raised bed gardens can be a great yard feature as the beds can be built to complement the existing landscaping. Raised beds are also great gardens for those with mobility issues as the beds can be built to any height, eliminating the need for constantly bending over or kneeling on the ground.

The growing environment of raised beds is easier to control. Raised beds generally require less weeding than ground gardens. If you live in a cooler climate, the soil in raised beds is easier to keep warm, so you can plant earlier in the spring and harvest later in the fall, extending your growing season beyond that of a traditional ground garden. And, you can fill your raised beds with pre-prepared, expertly mulched garden soil which will alleviate any soil problems your soil test revealed.

Like ground gardens, raised bed gardens have their disadvantages, too. Raised bed gardens are more expensive than in-ground gardens. The beds have to be constructed and a large amount of soil has to be purchased. Raised beds dry out more quickly, so they require more water than in-ground gardens. And, additional watering means additional fertilizing, since all that water is washing the nutrients from your soil more quickly.

The extra water also causes the soil to shrink and wooden beds to eventually break down, so soil will have to be added to the garden each year, and at some point, the beds will need to be replaced (approximately every 5-10 years depending on box material and climate).

When constructing a raised bed garden:

- Avoid using treated lumber.

  The chemicals in treated lumber can leach into the soil and into your garden's produce. Check the labels on any raised bed garden kits. If constructing your own raised beds, cedar and redwood work well as do landscape timbers.

You can also use a stone-based material for your garden, such as cinder blocks or chop stone. Some gardeners even pour cement borders for beds. Stone will keep the soil temperature warmer, so stone may not be an ideal material for those living in hot environments.

- Break up the ground beneath your raised beds.

  This is a must if your beds are shallow (under 1 foot) since your plant's roots will be anchoring themselves in the ground underneath your raised bed.

  If your beds are tall enough to support the plant's root system, you can skip this step, and you can line the bottom of the bed with newspaper or weed barrier to help cut back on weeds.

- Fill your garden beds with good quality soil.

  You're going to need a lot of garden soil to fill your raised beds and soil will likely be your priciest outlay for your new garden. Don't be tempted to skimp and use cheap topsoil. You'll have to add so much compost and fertilizer to get it up to par, you might as well have bought the more expensive garden soil to begin with. In fact, one seasoned gardener I know advises filling raised beds with just compost.

  There are a lot of soil calculators available online that can help you figure out just how much soil you need. Check out local large-scale landscape stores. They offer bulk garden soil and compost at far cheaper rates than buying soil by the bag.

  Fill your beds to the top, if not slightly overflowing. Once you begin watering, the soil will shrink.

- Consider drip irrigation for your raised beds.

  Yes, this is an additional gardening cost you can avoid if you need to. However, drip irrigation solves many of the watering problems associated with raised bed gardens.

Watering with a garden hose deluges the bed and leads to water washing out of the box, taking soil and minerals with it. The slow drip of an irrigation system allows the plants to soak up the water more efficiently, resulting in less runoff and less loss of soil.

Drip irrigation also helps prevent mold, mildew, and fungus from developing on plant leaves and fruit since irrigation systems water plants below leaves and blooms.

CHAPTER 3
SELECTING & PLANTING YOUR VEGETABLES: THE SEEDY PART OF GARDENING

Selecting Your Vegetables

You can grow most any vegetable in most any climate. However, the time of year you can plant that vegetable and the variety of that vegetable you can get to grow are heavily dependent on the climate you're growing that vegetable in. Peas will grow in northern and southern climates. But, if your garden is in the south, you need to plant heat tolerant pea varieties and plant them in the spring. Those with short growing seasons need to select early-to-harvest vegetable plants, like Early Xtra Sweet corn, Early Midget watermelons, and Green Comet broccoli.

So, how do you find out what vegetable varieties grow best in your area? Of course, the internet can be a good resource, but the amount of information spit back from a Google search can be overwhelming. Local garden resources are often a better bet as they can provide you with information specific to your region. They know what vegetables grow best. They're aware of any plant diseases or garden pests making the local rounds. They can advise you on common soil issues in your area. Your best local resources will be:

- Local agricultural colleges and universities.

  Many of these schools maintain webpages with regional gardening help and a list of vegetable plants that work well in your area. For example, if you live in Texas, Texas A&M's Aggie Horiculture website has a search tool that lets you find the best kinds of fruits and vegetables to grow in your county.

- Local greenhouses and nurseries.

  Unlike large chain stores, such as Home Depot, local nurseries will carry plants that grow best in your climate. Nursery plants are also better cared for and much more likely to survive and thrive after transplanting.

- City and county agricultural extension offices.

  These government offices can offer you pamphlets and advice about best planting practices in your area. They also provide soil tests for a small fee.

- Local garden clubs.

  Seek out garden clubs in your city and attend a few meetings to mingle with experienced gardeners. Most clubs are very welcoming to newcomers, and some even offer gardening seminars and classes for beginners.

- Local farmers markets.

If the produce is available at your local farmers market, you can grow it in your garden. Farmers markets are another great place to meet seasoned gardeners. These growers will also be up to speed on any seasonal plant and pest problems and can advise you accordingly.

Planting Your Crop

Once you've chosen the vegetables you're going to grow, there are three ways to get your plants in the ground: direct sowing, transplanting, and seed-starting.

Direct sowing is exactly what it sounds like: putting a seed directly into the ground. Some plants have to be directly sown. Corn, for example, doesn't transplant well. Generally, large seeds, like beans, peas, cucumbers, and melons can be directly sown. Root vegetables, like radishes, onions, and carrots, should also be directly sown.

To direct sow your plants:

1. Create rows or mounds per the seed pack directions. If the seeds will be sown in a row, make a furrow down the middle of the row to the planting depth recommended by the seed packet.

2. Sow the seeds according to package instructions. If the seeds are small, like carrots or onions, you can sprinkle them in your furrow. Sow large seeds, like corn, legumes, and squash, individually every 1"-3" in a row or 3-6 seeds per mound.

3. Water seeds consistently while they're germinating, but don't overwater. Soil should be moist but not soaking. If the soil is too dry, the seeds won't sprout. But, if the soil is kept too wet, the seeds will rot in the ground.

4. If the plants require trellising or supports, like pole beans or peas, put those in place now. If you wait until the plants are established, you risk damaging the roots when stakes are pushed into the ground.

5. Thin sprouted seedlings according to package directions. Thinning just means removing extraneous plants, so that your

remaining plants have 6"-12" of space between them. Don't be tempted to let all your plants develop; they can't grow properly in a confined space. You'll end up with strangled plants and little produce.

Plants are normally thinned when they develop secondary (true) leaves, or the plant reaches a certain height. For large seedlings, like corn or beans, trim the plant off at its stem base rather than pull it. If the thinned seedlings' roots have intertwined with the roots of the plant you intend to keep, you risk damaging that plant's roots if you pull the thinned one.

6. If you have a long growing season and want to harvest a continuous crop, stagger your seed plantings by two weeks. For example, sow two mounds of cucumbers now, two mounds of cucumbers two weeks later, and two mounds more two weeks after that.

Transplanting is taking an existing plant out of a container and putting it into the ground. Some vegetable seeds can't be sown directly. Tomatoes, peppers, and most herbs have to be started indoors and transplanted outdoors after they've been hardened off. You can start the seeds indoors yourself (which we'll discuss in a second), or you can buy the fully-formed plants from your local nursery.

When purchasing vegetable plants, select plants that look healthy. The plants should have green, perky leaves, not leaves that are brown, dry, or wilted. Try to pick plants without blooms and never buy a vegetable plant that's already producing. If a vegetable plant has already fruited, it's at the end of its production cycle and should have been transplanted long ago.

To transplant a plant:

1. Create a row or mound per the plant's label, and space the plants according the label's planting instructions, usually 18"-24".

2. Dig a hole deep enough in the ground that you will completely bury the plant's root ball.

3. Turn the plant upside down, and gently remove it from its container. Usually, the plant will slide right out. If not, gently tap the bottom of the container or gently squeeze the container's sides. Never yank a plant out by its stem.

   It's easier to transplant plants when they're damp, so water plants thirty minutes to an hour before transplanting. This also prevents the plant's soil from crumbling during transplant which can damage the plant's root system.

4. Gently loosen the plant's root ball. This will encourage the plant's roots to grow outward which better anchors the plant. Place the plant in the ground and fill in the area around the plant with soil. Lightly tamp the soil down. If the plants have any blooms, gently pinch them off.

5. If you live in a cool or windy climate, consider putting water walls or wind blocks around your plants for protection during their first few weeks in the ground. Large coffee cans with the tops and bottoms cut out work well.

6. Install tomato cages or support systems once water walls or wind blocks are removed. If you're not using water walls or wind blocks, install the cages when you transplant the plants.

Seed Starting

If you'd rather grow your tomatoes, peppers, and herbs from seed, start seeds indoors 6-12 weeks ahead of the last frost (the seed packet instructions will let you know exactly when). To start your seeds indoors, you'll need potting soil and seed-starting containers. Seed starting kits can be purchased at most garden supply stores, as can seed pots, peat pots, and black, plastic seed flats. You can also use small Dixie cups, empty egg cartons, or old ice cube trays with holes drilled for drainage.

To seed start your plants:

1. Fill seed-starting containers with moistened potting soil to a quarter inch from the top.

2. Place two to three seeds on top of the soil and cover with a fine layer of soil or peat moss to the planting depth recommended on the seed packet.

3. Water your new plantings using a spray bottle to keep seeds from washing out. Watering instructions are the same as for directly sown seeds: the seeds need to be kept moist but not soaking.

4. Keep your plants in a warm place. The tops of appliances work well. For faster germination, cover your containers with clear, plastic wrap. Remove the plastic once the first seeds sprout.

5. Once the plants have sprouted, move them to an area that gets good sunlight, like a south facing window. If you don't have a south facing window, you may need to invest in grow lights. If your new plants are too leggy, grow slowly, or don't develop true leaves, they're not getting enough sunlight.

6. Once the seedlings leaves are touching, it's time to thin. If you're going to pull the extra plants, do so when the soil is at its driest right before you water. If you've waited a little too long to thin because you temporarily succumbed to the temptation of keeping all of your seedlings, you can trim the extra plants off at the base of their stem.

7. Once outdoor temperatures are consistently warm enough to sustain your plants, you'll need to harden off your seedlings to get them used to living outdoors.

   Start by leaving the seedlings outside in a sunny (but not scorching), sheltered area for 3-4 hours. Gradually increase the plants' outdoor exposure by a few hours each day. After 7-10 days, you can transplant your new plants.

Extra seeds can be stored for up to a year. To best preserve seeds, keep them in the refrigerator, sealed in a moisture-proof container with a desiccant. Seeds won't germinate as well after storage, so you may find yourself replanting more stalled seeds than you did in the previous season.

CHAPTER 4
MOLD, MITES, AND
OTHER UNWANTED GUESTS:
MANAGING GARDEN PESTS & PLANT DISEASE

There are few things more frustrating than spending weeks weeding, watering, and tending your garden, only to emerge one morning and find half your tomato plants eaten to the stems by tomato worms. Or watching cucumber plants die one by one as their leaves become infected with a white mold you can't seem to control.

All gardeners have to be vigilant for signs of garden pests and plant diseases. These issues have to be contained early and quickly, or you risk massive crop infestations. This chapter provides some practical advice for handling common garden problems. But, you may be able to avoid many of these issues if you take a few preventative measures:

- Many plant problems stem from improper watering. Like seedlings, plants should be kept consistently moist but not soaking. The soil should feel damp to the touch an inch deep in the earth. Plants will need more water when they're small seedlings and later when they're producing. They'll also need more water when weather temperatures soar.

  Watch your plant's leaves; they'll let you know if you're overwatering or underwatering. Yellow leaves signal overwatering; wilted green or dry brown leaves are the result of underwatering.

  Water plants at the base of their stems, below leaves and blooms, to discourage mold or mildew from forming. Slow watering, drip irrigation systems do wonders in helping prevent plant problems that arise from watering issues.

- People who eat a healthy diet and maintain a good nutrient balance are better able to withstand infections. The same goes for plants, so routinely fertilize. Fertilizers are like plant vitamins, and fertilizing is especially important in raised bed gardening since plants eat up the contained soil nutrients quickly.

- Rotate crops each season, especially tomatoes and peppers. Tomato worms, the bane of tomato growers everywhere, lay their larvae in the soil just before winter. The larvae hatch and emerge in the spring and lay in wait for new tomato plants. I've also had tomato worms attack my peppers, but they tend to leave other vegetables alone.

- Keep garden beds clean and as weed-free as possible. Always remove fallen leaves. Pests like to hide under fallen leaves, and wet plant detritus encourages mold spores and mildew. Weeds sap water and nutrients from your vegetable plants, leaving them a little less healthy and a little more vulnerable to disease.

- Consider planting herbs, onions, garlic, and other pest-repelling plants, like marigolds and geraniums, around your vegetables. These strong smelling plants repel some pesty insects and harmful grubs. They also discourage rabbits, deer, and other animals.

- Encourage garden friendly bugs to hang around. Not all bugs are harmful to your plants; in fact, many can help you out. Carnivorous bugs, like spiders and ladybugs, aren't interested in your vegetables. They're interested in eating other bugs. Certain beetles feed on caterpillars and snails. And, wasps are a natural enemy of the dreaded tomato worm.

Pest Control

The type of pests you'll encounter will depend on the time of year, what you're growing, and the region you live in. Cutworms tend to be most active in May and June when plants are still low to the ground. If you're growing corn, you'll need to be on the lookout for corn earworms, but if you're lucky enough to live in an area that doesn't have raccoons, you won't have to worry about them raiding your corn patch. If you do live in an area that has raccoons, be prepared to launch full-scale counterattacks. Here are a few suggestions to dealing with garden pests:

- Small pests, like aphids, and other leaf eaters can be removed and deterred by routinely spraying plant leaves with soapy water. Mix ½ teaspoon of dish soap per quart of water.

- Immediately remove caterpillars from your plants and summarily execute them by dropping them into a container of soapy water. Many caterpillars, especially tomato worms, blend in with the plant they're noshing on, so they can be hard to spot.

  If large chunks of leaves are suddenly missing from your plant, you likely have a caterpillar lurking nearby. If it's not visible, give the plant a gentle shake and listen hard. Some caterpillars make a clicking noise when they're disturbed. You can use the noise to locate them and carry out their sentence.

- If snails or slugs are attacking your plants, you can lure them away with beer. Leave a saucer filled with beer in your problem snail areas (stale beer actually works best). The snails will crawl into the beer and drown.

- Placing barriers around your plants, like rocks or mulch, can also help deter slugs and snails as they don't like crawling over sharp objects. Barriers also discourage certain types of beetles.

- If plants are suddenly collapsing for no reason, you may have a vine weevil infestation. Vine weevil grubs, tiny white grubs with brown heads, are voracious eaters, and they can quickly destroy a plant's roots. Vine weevils are difficult to control, and you may have to resort to pesticides to get them out of your garden.

  If you are completely, totally, 100% against pesticides, some organic methods of removing nematodes, such as planting marigolds or leaving the land fallow for a season (unplanted), may help you control your vine weevil population.

- If wild animals are sneaking into your garden at night, try leaving a radio playing outside. Motion-sensored lights will also scare away some animals. Leaving human hair in your garden or using a predator-urine spray along the garden perimeter will similarly discourage animals.

- Spray ripening vegetables with a mix of soapy water, garlic powder, and chili. Animals won't like the smell or taste and will leave your produce alone.

- If squirrels, skunks, raccoons, rabbits, and other small varmints start becoming a large problem, consider live trapping and relocating the animals elsewhere.

Plant Diseases

Plants can get sick just like people can, and plants can infect neighboring plants, so it's important to deal with plant disease as soon as a plant starts showing signs of distress. Plants are subject to wilt, rot, mildew and fungus. Plants can also be infected by viruses and bacteria, though this is less common. Diseases can affect plant leaves, plant roots, and even the plant's fruit.

As with most things, an ounce of disease prevention is worth a pound of cure, so follow best watering and fertilizing practices when gardening to keep plants healthy and discourage disease. To control plant disease:

- Spray plant leaves spotted with mildew or mold with a mix of 1 teaspoon dish soap and 2-3 teaspoons baking soda per quart of water to control the infection.

- Water the soil and not the plant. This prevents water from standing on leaves and soil from splashing back on the plant, both of which encourage molds and fungi.

- Make sure plants have adequate spacing between them, so sunlight reaches plant leaves and air can property circulate. Tangled masses of leaves make it hard for water to evaporate and can lead to mold and mildew developing. This is another reason why thinning plants is so important.

- If you live in a humid area, you're going to experience more problems with plant disease. When deciding what vegetables to plant, consider using disease-resistant varieties.

- Don't forget to prune vegetable plants that require pruning, like tomatoes, and always use clean pruning shears. And, don't forget to stake plants that need staking, like pole beans and peas. Trellising vegetables that can be trained to grow on a trellis, like cucumbers, helps keep the plant leaves dry and clean, and thus, less likely to develop mold spores.

- Keep your garden clean. Remove dead and infected leaves and fruit. Weed prodigiously.

- Be on the lookout for late blight, a serious fungal disease that affects tomatoes and potatoes. I'm sure you've heard of Ireland's famous potato famine? Well, late blight was their source of all the angst.

The leaves of affected plants will have black spots with white spores. Late blight cannot be cured and can take out your entire crop quickly, so pull infected plants. In fact, if a plant is heavily infected with any disease, it's usually a good idea to pull it.

- Some plant diseases are caused by nutrient imbalances in the soil. Blossom end rot, a disease that affects the plant's fruit, is caused by a calcium deficiency. Keeping soil adequately fertilized will prevent many plant problems.

- Never compost infected plants, or you risk infecting your entire garden during the next growing season. Also, never harvest seeds from infected plants. Consider leaving any heavily infected garden patches fallow for a year.

CHAPTER 5
BRINGING IN THE HARVEST:
GARDENING AFTER THE GROWING SEASON
ENDS

You tested your soil, added the right amount of compost and nutrients to get it up to snuff, kept your garden watered and weeded, and kept your plants happy and healthy. Now, you have a bumper crop.

Maybe a little too bumper.

You've run out of recipe ideas for green beans, you eat sliced cucumbers with every meal, and while your children are not normally picky eaters, they did balk when you handed them a bowlful of peas covered in milk for breakfast.

When vegetable plants start producing, they usually start producing in a big way, and you can find yourself trying to find uses for crates of produce. You don't want to see the food go to waste; you've put a lot of effort into growing it. But, there are only so many ears of corn your family can eat, and there are only so many tomatoes you can pawn off on co-workers, neighbors and friends. You may want to explore methods of preserving food.

The idea of food preservation scares a lot of gardeners. It shouldn't. It's relatively easy. Often, it's easier than getting the vegetables to grow in the first place. Plus, you'll have the luxury of home grown produce year around. It's difficult to go back to store-bought produce in the winter after you've tasted fresh grown vegetables in the summer. Consider:

- Low acid vegetables, like corn, peas, beans, and peppers, freeze well. Always blanch produce before freezing.

- Vegetable stocks also freeze well as do soups and chilies.

- Fresh herbs can be dried and stored for later use.

- Highly acidic tomatoes are fairly easy to can, as are spaghetti sauces and tomato-based salsas.

- Cucumbers, okra, and cabbage can be pickled. The high concentration of vinegar in the brine makes these vegetables easy for beginners to can, as well.

- Most other vegetables can be preserved through pressure canning.

Always follow best food safety practices when canning or freezing produce. For a more comprehensive guide to food preservation, please consult our "Homestead Cooking" guide.

Winterizing Your Garden

You've picked all your corn. Your tomatoes are done producing. The weather forecast is predicting the first autumn frost three nights from now. You're done gardening for the year, right?

Well, gardeners can actually look at fall one of two ways: the end of the gardening season or, more productively, the beginning of the next gardening season. If you take a little time to winterize your garden in the fall, it will pay off big when you replant crops in the spring.

Gardeners have different ways of preparing their garden for winter. Some gardeners till their garden soil in the fall. Other gardeners add compost and mulch to their beds. Some gardeners plant cover crops. And, some just pick their last vegetable and walk away, forgetting about the whole mess until spring.

- Regardless of how you plan to winterize your garden, all spent vegetable plants should be pulled at the end of the growing season. If the plants were healthy, they can be left on top of the soil to decompose, or they can be added to your mulch pile.

  If the plants were unhealthy and showing signs of disease, they should be removed, thrown away, and disavowed.

- The impetus behind winterizing a garden is protecting the garden soil. Soil that is left unplanted and untended will erode, and you'll lose vital soil and nutrients.

  For large garden plots, consider planting a winter cover crop, like clover, rye, or winter wheat to keep garden soil in place. An added bonus of these crops is that they'll keep winter weeds to a minimum. In the spring, the cover crop can be tilled into the soil for an instant green fertilizer (more commonly known as "green manure").

  Small garden plots also benefit from cover crops. However, if you're working with a small amount of space, you can also cover your beds with mulch. Similar to cover crops, mulch will protect your soil from erosion and discourage weeds. Straw and wood chips work well as a small bed cover.

- Some gardeners fertilize in the fall. Others choose not to, believing the nutrition gained is lost during the winter's precipitation. Some gardeners hedge their bets, and work compost into the soil in both fall and spring.

  Whatever side of the autumn mulching debate you fall on, just remember: if you're planting a cover crop, it's a good idea to give it some nutrition to establish itself on.

- If you live in a warmer climate, you may be able to grow vegetables year around. In fact, some vegetables, like lettuce or other leafy greens, may only grow in your climate during winter months.

  If you live in cool, northern climates, it still may be possible to garden in the winter. However, it will require a little infrastructure in the form of hoop houses and garden covers.

- Consider using the winter to evaluate your past garden. What plants grew well? Which plants didn't? Do you think certain plants would have done better if they were planted in a different area of your garden? Were there vegetables you wish you'd tried? Are there vegetables you wished you planted more of? Or less of? Do you wish you'd configured your garden differently?

  Once you've identified what you liked about your garden (or what you didn't), you'll have a better idea of the adjustments you can make for the next growing season.

- If you had a particularly bad pest infestation, especially any type of grub, fall would be a great time to aggressively treat the issue. Also, tilling the soil in the fall will help destroy the larvae of some insidious garden pests, like tomato worms.

- You can elect to leave your garden alone until the spring. Just know, you'll have a lot more work to do to get your garden prepared for planting.

CONCLUSION

Congratulations! You now have the know-how to successfully start your vegetable garden. You know where you're planting your garden, how you're going to protect it, and what type of garden you're going to have: a ground garden or a raised bed garden. You've gotten your soil tested (you have, right?), have seeds and plants ready to go, and soon you'll be harvesting homegrown vegetables.

Before we part, I want to leave you with a final piece of advice. When selecting your plants and seeds, consider buying non-GMO (genetically modified) varieties. These seeds and plants are provided by companies who have signed the Safe (non-GMO) Seeds Pledge and are committed to organic farming practices, preventing ecological contamination, and preserving biodiversity. Likely, you're trying to keep your garden as natural as possible, so you'll want to select non-GMO vegetables anyway. Most local greenhouses and nurseries carry non-GMO seed and plant varieties.

I hope you've enjoyed our time together, covering the basics of vegetable gardening. I'm sure you're ready to get started, so I'll leave you to your planting.

Good luck and happy gardening.

www.ingramcontent.com/pod-product-compliance
Lightning Source LLC
Chambersburg PA
CBHW070134290526
45789CB00005B/2238